THE
RADIANT
KINGDOM

An allegorical study
of meditation

The RADIANT KINGDOM

An allegorical study
of meditation

by Ian Macwhinnie

CELESTIAL ARTS

First published in Great Britain in 1994 by Benwell Books,
155 Clifton Road, Rugby CV21 3QN, Warwickshire

Celestial Arts
P.O. Box 7123
Berkeley, California 94707

Cover and text designed by Victor Ichioka

Library of Congress Cataloging-in-Publication Data

Macwhinnie, Ian.
    The radiant kingdom : an allegorical study of meditation / by
Ian Macwhinnie
        p.   cm.
    ISBN 0-89087-789-0 (alk. paper)
    1. Meditations.   2. Allegory.   I. Title
BL627.M32   1996
291.4'3—dc20   95-47990
                                                        CIP

Printed in United States of America

1   2   3   4 - 98   97   96

PREFACE

This book is an attempt to set the various meditation practices, most of them derived from Asian culures, in a context which has meaning and value to the analytical bent of the Western mind, without losing the magic, mystery, and grace of these ancient traditions in the process.

The Eastern model of the mind, based to a great extent on an observation of its functioning in meditation, is very different from current Western theories of psychology and psychoanalysis. As such, they may appear to be mutually impenetrable. The Western mind finds it difficult to understand Eastern thought, especially with the presence of words and concepts which have no direct equivalent in European languages. Eastern traditions also fail to appreciate the levels of stress which are taken as normal in the West, and their literature does not make allowances for it. Curiously, it is this aspect of stress reduction that has prompted the widening of interest in meditation throughout Europe and North America, even though it only scratches the surface of the range of potential benefits to be derived from practicing meditation.

My hope is that, armed with a greater understanding of the processes involved in meditation, more people will be encouraged to persevere and reap the benefits of a practice which is enjoyable, rewarding and nourishing.

AUTHOR'S NOTE

This book begins with a fairy tale, a traditional method of shedding light on the mysteries of life and describing the activities of the subconscious in an entertaining and engaging manner. I hope that the archetype created by the story makes it easier to follow the more analytical descriptions of the mind in meditation which follow.

At the end of the book is an appendix, A Brief History of the Universe, which may at first sight seem irrelevant, but in reality outlines the touchstone and goal of all meditative activity, which is to bring us back into full conscious realization of our divine heritage. A tall order, but I am sure the rewards will repay any effort expended!

Contents

THE
RADIANT
KINGDOM

O NCE UPON A TIME, THERE
was a radiant King who ruled over a radiant kingdom, with peace and prosperity in every corner of his land. His palace was at the center of the city and from it spread long, wide avenues lined with trees bearing all manner of fruits. Outside the city were tall mountains and rivers that ran with pure water. There were forests with every kind of tree and lakes full of beautiful flowers. All different kinds of creatures inhabited the kingdom. Many animals roamed the land and performed all number of useful functions. Music constantly filled the air and nobody was ever hungry. Apart from humans, there were advisers and helpers drawn from the angelic realms who all took part in carrying out the King's wishes and commands.

The chief of the King's advisers was called Whisper. His main role was to pass on the King's commands to all the other helpers and workers so that order and beauty were maintained throughout the kingdom. He had this name because of the quiet and unobtrusive way in which he carried out his work. In fact, he went about giving his commands in such a subtle way that nobody could actually recall ever having seen him. The only one whom we can be sure knew him face to face was the King himself. Nevertheless, he was widely honoured and his commands were always treated as if they came directly from the King himself, which of course, they had. It was because of Whisper's work that happiness and harmony were maintained in the land. To help in this, he had under him all the artists and musicians whom he inspired and who made sure there was always music being played and beautiful paintings and sculptures to be seen and enjoyed.

Another of the King's most important helpers was called Brains. He was a very precise fellow, who liked things to be known for exactly what they were and that is why he insisted on being called Brains, even though others may have liked to given him a more poetic name. Whenever any planning of new buildings or canals had to be done, Brains would draw up the plans and supervise all the construction right down to the very last detail. Or, if the King wanted to travel anywhere in his kingdom, Brains would make sure all the arrangements were properly in place. Along with his teams of helpers, he played a very important role in the day to day running of the kingdom and, though he wasn't lovable in the way one ordinarily thinks of the word—and he probably would have disapproved if he thought he was—everyone respected and appreciated him. Brains received his instructions from Whisper with whom he worked very closely and would always report back anything he thought was useful about the decisions which had been made and often made valuable suggestions himself, though this wasn't his strong point.

Although there were many animals in the kingdom, there was one particular favorite of the court. This was a monkey called Watchout, whom everyone loved because of his frisky and excitable nature. He wasn't a particularly useful animal though he did spend a lot of time with Brains, especially when there was work being done. Because of his nervous and fearful disposition, he was always looking for something to go wrong and many times he helped to ward off an accident by shouting, "Watch out!" in time to stop someone being hurt during heavy construction work. In fact he used to shout, "Watch out!" so often, even when there was no need, that eventually everyone laughingly gave that to him as his name. At other times, Watchout would roam all over the kingdom—he especially liked the border regions of the country—looking out for some danger which he could then warn everybody about and gain their attention. Although well loved, he was also treated with amusement because he would jump at the tiniest thing, even when there was no need, and often give everyone else a fright too. But it was all taken in good sport.

For many hundreds of years, the King ruled peacefully over his beautiful kingdom. All his subjects were happy and fulfilled and no one could even remember a time when things had been less than perfect. The King spent most of his time either on his throne in the room where he met with his chief ministers, or in a room behind which he would usually occupy at night. Still, even at night, the doors of this room were not closed and the King's radiance, which was in fact the source of the radiance of the whole land and everyone's happiness and prosperity, still shone through and breathed its life into everything.

But then things began to change, slowly at first, and then more and more. It started when enemies began to appear on the borders of the kingdom, small groups of bandits and robbers and eventually a big army, which required all the efforts of the King and his people to defeat. The first news of these invasions was brought by Watchout, who had been wandering, as was his habit, on the frontiers of the kingdom. At first, the news was brought back to Whisper who consulted with the King and they tried to resolve these conflicts by peaceful means. Unfortunately, as more and more enemies appeared, Watchout only went as far as telling Brains about them and they began to deal with the problem between them. They decided to defend their kingdom by force and started creating an army to beat back the attackers. Watchout brought all the other monkeys from around the country to help keep watch on the borders and be alert for danger and Brains turned his helpers into soldiers. As their enemies became more numerous, Watchout and Brains increased the size of their army until there were more helpers and workers fighting than there were doing their usual jobs.

After this state of affairs had continued for some time, Watchout and Brains decided that it would be best if they took control of the kingdom themselves. So one day, with a group of soldiers, they attacked the palace and took control of it. They put the King and Whisper into the room behind the throne and locked it from the outside. Because the door was locked, the King's radiance could no longer shine over the country and Whisper's gentle advice and help could not be heard through the locked door.

Once this had happened, things went from bad to worse in the kingdom. All the beauty in the land disappeared. The fruit trees were not as plentiful as before and people went hungry. The music stopped and, without Whisper's inspiration, all his helpers disappeared into the rocks and stones where they could no longer be heard or seen. This sorry state of affairs was increasingly to the liking of Brains and Watchout. They even started to spread it around that the King and Whisper had never existed and the memories of radiance and joyfulness of the past were just dreams.

All the efforts of the kingdom were now turned to defending the country against enemies and, the larger the army became, the more enemies there seemed to be. And all this time, the state of the kingdom worsened. With so many people fighting in the army or making new weapons, there were hardly enough left to look after the ordinary everyday things. Buildings went to wrack and ruin, the roads became pitted and potholed, and there was hardly enough to eat.

But Brains and Watchout still thought they were doing the right thing in order to make their country safe. Even when the enemies had all been defeated, Watchout was not content to put his mind to other things. If anything, he was even more nervous and fearful than before. He could say that his fears were justified and there was good reason to be on guard all the time. At the same time, he also thought he was now a very important character and, with Brains's encouragement, he even used to go and sit on the King's throne. Brains also thought that his colleague was very important. He took his orders from Watchout and was in charge of everything there was to do. He didn't mind that Watchout was only a monkey and he wasn't really able to tell whether the fearful and silly orders he received were good ones or not. At least they were instructions of some sort, which kept him busy and, more than anything else, Brains liked to be busy.

This state of affairs had been continuing for a very long time, when one day there appeared on the edge of the kingdom a beautiful Queen surrounded by many advisers and helpers, who seemed to make the whole countryside around her glow with brightness. Watchout and his monkey helpers had, of course, seen her from some way off and had sounded the alert for enemies approaching. By the time the Queen had arrived at the border, there was a large army waiting to meet her. But the Queen made no effort to enter the kingdom and anyway, she didn't have any soldiers with her. The army of the kingdom didn't make a move to attack because they wouldn't go outside their own borders. There was just the fearful noise of thousands of monkeys screeching and screaming and rushing back and forth announcing danger. However, the Queen didn't seem to mind. She seemed happy to stay where she was, despite the noise, and started to pitch her pavilions and tents as if she were getting ready to settle in for a long stay.

For a long while nothing happened. The Queen and her party made themselves comfortable where they were and the noise of monkeys screeching along the battlements continued day and night. Watchout and Brains were very confused as to what to do about the situation, since nothing like it had ever happened before. Previously, when enemies came, they tried to invade and had to be repelled. This was the first time anyone had just come up to the edge of their territory and waited there.

Slowly, however, the noise of the monkeys decreased as they began to get used to the presence of their visitors, who still made no attempt to enter the kingdom. Watchout himself started to become curious about what these people wanted, even though Brains advised against trying to get too friendly. Once the monkeys had stopped their fearful screeching, it was possible to hear more of the sounds from the tents and see more of what was going on. It seemed that their visitors were very happy and there was always music being played. Flowers began to bloom around the tents and even wild animals would come up very close to where the tents were pitched.

The atmosphere reminded Watchout and Brains of something they had long forgotten—a distant memory of some great happiness—though to start with they could not place it. One day, the two of them even went together out of their own territory to take a closer look at what was going on. They were invited to come in and see the Queen with whom they had a long and interesting conversation. The Queen told them many stories that were full of wisdom and the two of them became very quiet as they listened. They began to visit every day and started to become good friends. Watchout even found he could relax a bit in the presence of the Queen, something he had never been very good at, but hadn't been able to do at all since the King had been locked up. He could hardly remember as far back as that now, though the Queen's presence was slowly jogging his memory to recall the happy times of the past.

One day the Queen asked if she might come into the kingdom for a visit. At first Watchout and his horde of monkeys put up a lot of resistance to the idea and for a few days they were screeching and calling just as they did when the Queen first arrived. But in the end, the trust that had built up with the Queen, and the fact that everyone really felt very comfortable in her presence, made their minds up for them. On the journey to the palace, the Queen noticed how run down everything was and asked if it had always been that way. "Oh no," said Watchout and began telling the Queen all about the old days when the King was on his throne and peace and harmony reigned. The Queen asked if she might meet the King and, when they came to the palace, Watchout and Brains agreed that they too would like to see the King, whom they had forgotten completely about, once more.

The three of them went up to the throne room and up to the bolted door where the King and Whisper were imprisoned. They had been there so long that the bolts of the door had become completely rusted and stuck. They had to wait while Brains' workers broke down the doors. But when the King and Whisper came out, they looked just as fresh as when they had first been locked up. Straightaway, the King's radiance started to shine through the palace and make itself felt throughout the kingdom. Whisper's helpers felt the change almost immediately. They came out of their rocks and hiding places and music began to fill the air once more.

There was still much work to be done to restore everything to its former state, but everyone was glad the King was back and all worked hard on the repair work. Once they saw how quickly things improved, Watchout and Brains were only too glad to return to the roles they had before. The first things they did were to take charge of knocking down all the battlements on the borders of the country and to invite the rest of the Queen's followers to come and live in the palace.

The King and Queen seemed to know each other well and were very happy at being reunited. Within a few weeks they were married and ruled together over the kingdom. Once again, happiness and harmony reigned in the kingdom, the rivers flowed, the birds sang and every day was a celebration. Those who could remember how life was before the King was locked up said that, with their new Queen, things were, if anything, even better.

– The End –

DEThRONING
The
MONKEY

*In examining the allegorical aspects of the
fairy tale, we take up the story at the point
where the King has been imprisoned within
his castle, and Brains and the Monkey, Watchout,
have taken control. The work of meditation
is to release the King, our Innermost Self or
Soul, and set Brains and the Monkey to
useful productive activity which is within
the scope of their specific talents.*

1. THE AIM OF MEDITATION

MEDITATION AS A DELIBERATE, conscious practice has formed part of the cultures of most civilizations on earth. It is a most valuable tool in helping us towards greater knowledge of ourselves, first as individuals and personalities and then as spiritual beings with a rightful and important place in this Divine Universe. Meditation can be done simply for relaxation and the general benefits to health this brings. This is, however, only the first stage of what is essentially a spiritual practice carried out on the principle that, underlying our personalities and the activities of the senses, there is something more constant, more real, and more eternal. This has been described in various spiritual traditions as the soul, ego, spirit, atman, Universal Mind, the Christ within, and many other terms. This soul is understood to inhabit a world which is seen as the origin of the creative or causative forces behind everyday reality. It had its existence before the birth of our physical bodies ("Before Abraham was, I am" —*The Gospel According to St John*, Ch.8 v.58) and, by extension, continues its existence after death. The gift and joy of meditation lies in its potential to open our awareness to the experience of this world of the soul.

The attractions of the material world, of wealth and possessions, can never be completely enjoyed if the source of happiness has not been discovered within ourselves. We can ask, when we are happy, where do these feelings actually come from? They most certainly do not come from the

objects or experiences which are the apparent cause of acti-
vating these "happiness-juices." Our feelings of happiness, or
any other emotion for that matter, spring up from somewhere deep in us. Exterior events are only a catalyst to allow
us to experience them. A full and complete happiness can
only be possible when there is a sense of connection to that
which is deepest in us, the source itself, the soul. Without this
integration, all our enjoyments will be tinged with those
unresolved fears and feelings that arise from not really being
in touch with ourselves. And as humans, what is not known
is generally seen as something to be feared.

This dualistic notion of being separated from ourselves
is, fortunately, more apparent than real. It is like two sides of a
coin which are each unaware that they are irretrievably
bound to the other and cannot be separated. The full reality is
that both sides of the coin are necessary, the existence of one
side immediately implies the existence of the other and,
taken together, they make up something much greater than
each could be on its own. Our logical tendency to break
everything down into its component parts misleads us into
believing that there is an "everyday self" on the one hand
and a "soul" on the other, which don't seem to have much
apparent relation to each other. The practice of meditation
brings these two aspects into closer relation so that all the bits
and pieces can start to fit together to form a coherent and
integrated whole. As the value of this experience seeps into
our daily lives through regular practice, it is common to find
that unproductive thoughts and feeling patterns disappear of
their own accord, and are replaced with a greater sense of
wholeness and harmony in ourselves.

This process of the soul awakening, or rather of us
awakening to the soul, takes place in our very essence,
beyond thought and speech and feelings. It is often a long
time before people really notice the changes. Adjustments

and improvements are taking place at all levels of our being, physiological, chemical, in the endocrine system, they are going on in cellular structure at the deepest levels of our being. It may happen that one wakes up one day and notices that old habits and thought patterns have gone away by themselves, unnoticed and unmissed.

Not only humans, but nearly all animals and insects could be said to practice a form of meditation in their ability to remain motionless for hours at a time, to just be what they are when there is no particular pressure to be doing anything else. The praying mantis, for example, sacred to the Bushmen of southern Africa, takes up an apparent posture of prayer for hours at a time if circumstances allow. This ability to be what-one-most-naturally-is is, at the simplest and most complete level of experience, the goal of meditation. In Zen understanding, it is to know one's "original face."

Taken in its widest sense, the meditative process includes contemplation and prayer and can be extended to include chanting, singing, dancing, ritual, and other natural expressions of the human spirit's exuberance. Listening to music can also take us through repose and relaxation to a timeless state where the usual restless, churning activity of the Monkey Mind is suspended. Seen from a spiritual viewpoint, these aim to achieve the same goals as meditation: to come to a deeper sense of connection with ourselves.

THE
SEARCH
FOR THE
KING

2. TRADITIONS OF MEDITATION

LL MEDITATIVE TECHNIQUES
share this common aim of bringing the everyday chattering
mind—the main controlling force in our lives—into a receptive state, by allowing it to quiet down. The goal of meditation is finally achieved when the mind can spontaneously
maintain this steadiness whatever the outer circumstances,
when an inner calm pervades all our activities, however turbulent. This is not something that will be readily achievable
by most of us without a considerable amount of time and
effort, nevertheless, some of the quality of this experience can
start to flow into our lives from the start of practising meditation. The meditative state can be achieved and continued in
singing, dancing, or any other activity and can be practiced in
any position. It is not absent, so to speak, from any of the
Buddha's four postures of walking, sitting, lying, and standing.

Meditation is essentially a receptive process. The meditator is opening up to forms and forces which exist, in a figura-
tive sense, beyond or behind the normal everyday mind.
These can be experienced in terms of feelings and perceptions as a deeper sense of happiness, fulfillment and self-
knowledge. To be able to hear what is moving more deeply
within us (to become open to the impulses and messages
from Whisper in the story), the mind needs to become less
"noisy" or dominant, just as, in a room full of noise and chattering people, it is difficult to hear someone whispering
softly. The thinking or experiencing faculties need to be

quiet and steady for the process of spiritual unfoldment to begin.

The strongest traditions of meditation come to us from the Asian cultures, from Buddhism, particularly in its Tibetan and Zen forms, and Hinduism. Other religious traditions have included meditative practices in their methods of worship. There is an implicit history of meditation in the experiences of Christianity's mystics, where the use of prayer in monastic settings merges into more contemplative modes. We have the remarkable testimony of its saints who have forged a path of their own towards realization of the Godhead. We do not, however, have very much in the way of techniques which can be handed on and employed practically by others. Some of these practices, drawn largely from Eastern traditions, have, in recent years, been widely adopted in the West, often in modified or diluted form, as ways of reducing the stress and tension that result from daily life. Basic techniques of stilling the mind are widely recommended simply as a method of relaxation rather than with any specific aim of increasing self-knowledge or understanding.

The literature of the East is full of marvellous insight into the relationship of individual mind to Universal Mind. The Buddhist and Hindu texts contain enormous value as inspiring poetry and practical tuition to support the pilgrim on his way. Nevertheless, they speak to an audience with a quite different view of life from our own, a culture with different priorities and understanding. Taoist and Zen works, complete and magnificent in themselves, offer little in the way of practical benefit to the Western mind, which naturally resists the approach to life found in these writings. For example, the Taoist concept of *wu-wei*, loosely translated as "going with the flow," may even be interpreted as a recipe for disaster by the Western mind, which likes to have everything ordered and under control.

Even with a willingness to explore Eastern teachings, a considerable amount is lost in the translation and, without an appreciation of the East's fundamental insights into the nature of the mind, it is difficult to find anything of practical value in these texts. It may be that the Eastern approach presupposes a basic understanding, almost imbibed with mother's milk, to which the Western mind no longer has access. What is certain is that errors of understanding do creep in when attempting to convey the meaning of specific concepts relating to a worldview so foreign from our own. Words and phrases which have no direct equivalent in English are absorbed into our language with only the vaguest notion of what is being referred to.

Regardless of our ability to comprehend these teachings, either Eastern or Western, we all have within ourselves the key to understanding their underlying principles. Each of us is equipped with the mind, intelligence, feelings, and senses necessary to take the path ourselves. Nothing is able to replace our own faculties and capacity for experience. These teachings, however profound they may be in all cultures, are in the last analysis simply guideposts for us on our own inner journey of self-exploration and self-understanding. We will hear an affirming echo within us when something stated in a book resonates with a truth we have discovered, even half-consciously, ourselves.

This is not say that there will not be benefit from gaining as wide a theoretical understanding as possible. A tour of some foreign city, for example, is likely to be more enjoyable and instructive if we have obtained maps in advance and gained some idea of what we are likely to encounter. Likewise, before embarking upon the practice of meditation, it is as well to develop some understanding of the mind and its nature. Then the practices which we carry out, the various meditation styles and techniques we use, will have a more meaningful context and, hopefully, be of greater value.

Many people have started to meditate but have given up because their first or early experiences have not been as glorious and earth-shattering as the promotional literature implied they would. Without a framework for understanding their experiences, they naturally became discouraged. Entering a dark and unfamiliar terrain, armed with only a candle, it is not unnatural to want to turn back when the light starts to flicker or appears to go out.

The next section aims to provide a basic map of the terrain which may be encountered in meditation, and provide a context for understanding the many different types of experience which may come up.

3. UNDERSTANDING THE MIND

T HE EVOLUTION OF LIFE FROM its spiritual origins into matter has been a process of ever-increasing differentiation. The Spirit, in its original indivisible state, became the many. From the multiplication of single-celled organisms, the whole variety of plant, insect, and animal life (up to and including humanity itself) came into existence. Human beings, with the unique ability to think for themselves, have continued this process of dividing things and separating them. This work of the intellectual faculty has not only been applied in the sciences, by isolating objects and events for the purpose of studying them, it has also been turned inward on our own selves. The inner world of the individual has been divided by psychologists into various boxes such as mind, body, brain, ego, intuition, id, emotions, feelings, and so on. These are then further subdivided. The emotions are compartmentalized into love, hate, guilt, the feelings into good, bad, and ugly, etc. We are the divided self.

These divisions have their uses, certainly. If I have a pain somewhere in my body, it is likely to be more difficult to get help if I cannot explain that it is my leg and not my feelings that are injured. An examination of all these differences shows, however, that they are more apparent than real. For a start, something that affects one part has its repercussions in other parts. If I hurt my body, my emotions and feelings will certainly be affected and the pain may be such that it is difficult to think with my brain at all. Whenever one aspect of ourselves is being emphasized, all other parts are involved.

To make progress in meditation we must begin to think of ourselves once more as a whole. Even if we are practicing, say, a devotional meditation from the heart, our mind, body, emotions, and intuition are all taking part in the process to a greater or lesser degree. It is, perhaps, likely that meditators in the East would naturally assume this interconnectedness and not think that one aspect could be developed or emphasized or studied without reference to the others. In the West, we have the idea that each part can be treated individually and microscopically without reference to the other parts or to the whole.

Part of the general confusion around meditation in the West results from translating Eastern texts while maintaining a Western "mind-set," trying to force a round peg into a square hole. Eastern concepts cannot be approached with the idea that they will fit into the categories of Western psychoanalytical thought. To add to the difficulties, conceptual terms generally have a much broader range of meaning than we are familiar with in the English language. In any one instance, however, some aspects of the concept may be being emphasized more than other. Only the context will reveal the true meaning. This has been the cause of many of the difficulties of both translating and understanding Eastern teachings. For example, the Chinese word *hsin*, used in Buddhist texts, is generally translated as "mind" though sometimes, depending on the translator's interpretation of the context, as "heart." To the Chinese, however, *hsin* generally signifies both "heart-and-mind" and sometimes, depending on the context, much more. The whole perceptive faculty is often indicated.

In the practice of meditation, we are aiming for a unity of perception. The fragmentation of the everyday personality must be reabsorbed into its natural wholeness for us to begin to enter the essentially unified world of the soul. Whatever technique we are using, we are aiming to create a single organ which includes everything that is part of our normal awareness: thoughts, emotions, the senses, sensations, and will. This is our *hsin*, our heart-mind.

So, for this book, whenever the word "mind" is used in relation to meditation, it can be understood to include all those aspects which make up the conscious perceptive faculty, through which we experience ourselves and the world around us. In meditation, these are all involved and are brought into their proper relationship with each other. They each know their place and appreciate there is a time to be silent and still, as well as a time to be active and outgoing. For example, in the stillness of pure meditation, the emotions will be awake and present, but not active except as a will towards the experience. If the emotional nature were not participating, even though the meditator is not "being emotional," it could not take part in the transformations which are happening. All aspects and faculties are involved, acting as receptors for new energy which can transform them, improve their functioning and, as a result, benefit the general quality of life.

These changes also extend to the body since, as the mind settles down in meditation, the physiology is also automatically affected. The rest allowed to the nervous system makes it possible for healing to be carried on at a deeper level than is reached even in sleep. This has been shown by comparative measurements of heart rate and blood pressure. For this reason, meditation can be practiced simply for relaxation, without any specific spiritual goals in mind. Among many possible physical improvements, there may be a corrective influence on posture, as the body becomes more relaxed. The back will of its own accord start to straighten so that it can remain unsupported for longer periods. As tension leaves the neck and shoulders, the neck itself may appear to straighten and lengthen. Tension stored in the muscles of the legs will be dissolved and the knees, in a crossed-legs position, will be able to fall slowly to the floor. Many other physical benefits associated with reduced tension and improved physiological functioning can bring improvements to daily life.

4. THE MONKEY MIND

T HE EASTERN MIND HAS
viewed life from a perspective of wholeness and integration,
while the Western approach has been to dissect and submit to
the rigours of the microscope. We have seen how great is the
potential for misunderstanding that arises in translating
Eastern concepts into Western ways of thinking. Without
comparable terms, much of value is lost and it is hard for
those with a Western background and education to apply
these teachings to any advantage. One encouraging note,
though, is that there is no inherent difference between the
occidental and oriental mind. The same faculties and poten-
tials are there, only the application of them has been different. But in order to understand what is involved in the
meditation process, we need to recognize and accept the different ways that the mind has developed in the East and West.

Westerners tend to suffer from an over-active intellectual focus. We can say that, certainly as far as Eastern teachers of
meditation are concerned, they have not had the same
difficulty. The problem does not perhaps exist to the same
extent for people who have tended to see life as a whole—as
something essentially integrated. As a result, the problem fac-
ing Westerners, of starting meditation from an over-stimulat-
ed intellectual faculty, is not very well covered.

Nevertheless, we need to make use of the mental faculty
to gain some insight into the meditation process. Without an
understanding of the how and why of meditation, it will be

difficult to make headway, especially when faced with the additional difficulties that arise from the translation process.

First, we need to get a clear perception of the role and function of the intellect in limiting our awareness of ourselves as whole and integrated. This aspect of the divided self is responsible for splitting our essential wholeness into its various parts, though we can still acknowledge the part the intellect or concrete mind has had to play in the development of humanity, especially in terms of the scientific and material achievements we enjoy the benefit of today. On its own, the intellect is merely inquisitive. It wants to look into everything, take it all apart and put it back together again. It is not malicious or "judgemental" and, as with Brains in the story, has no real moral sense. It is very useful for comprehending instruction manuals, reading maps, and other analytical tasks. Its tendency to separate and divide, however, works exactly against the process of greater integration which we aim to cultivate through meditation.

There is, however, an aspect of the intellect which is not nearly so neutral in its interest. This can be understood as the "monkey mind," which evaluates all that the intellect has divided. Its overriding interest is control of the whole individual and its response to events, both interior and exterior. It wishes to rule over all other aspects of the personality within a narrow framework, which is set by its own limitations. It supports the agenda of the intellect and vice-versa, since it is an aspect of it, but denies space to all other elements of the individual which it cannot understand, particularly the emotions, feelings, intuition, and sensing faculties. The main way it enforces control over these attributes is by denying the validity of any experience gained through them. The monkey mind is afraid that its ability to keep things safe, under control and within the narrow limits it has set for itself will be undermined.

Similarly, it fights hard against all change. What is unknown is to be feared as a threat to its ability to adapt and cope and, ultimately, to its own existence. The name, monkey mind, derives first from this timidity and, secondly, from one of its main ways of maintaining control in the personality. This is by setting up a constant and random motion which does not allow any rest or stillness. In this way, it prevents the opening up of receptivity so one can just observe, or be with, the flow of thoughts, feelings, and observations with all judgement suspended. The monkey mind interposes a continuous stream of comments, judgements and irrelevant thoughts to throw sand in the face of any other experience which may be coming along to threaten its control. How often have you been having a pleasurable or novel experience only to hear your thoughts chattering along endlessly about something completely disconnected to the present situation? This is the monkey mind talking, controlling the amount of pure experience which is open to you so that its tenure as Monkey King is not threatened.

The monkey mind has been identified in part by modern psychologists as the "flight-or-fight" response. The theory is that this response developed as a faculty very early in the life of humanity in its struggle for everyday survival. Compared to other animals on the prehistoric stage, humans were poorly equipped in terms of physical advantages over other predators. The only advantage which humans had over other creatures was the ability to think and make elective decisions. Faced with danger, humans could quickly weigh up the situation and decide whether to engage in battle or run for it. It is likely that, since a human would nearly always be at a physical disadvantage in a contest with a predator, the most usual response would be to flee. In other words a "No!" to the situation.

This response became so important to the survival of the species—in fact survival could be said to have depended on it —that the monkey mind quickly assumed a position as lord over all the other faculties, becoming the precursor of the dominant scientific and analytical culture we live in. In addition, this "No!" was such an effective weapon against predators that the monkey mind which, as we can see, has very little imagination, decided to make use of it as the main way of being in control, even when life-threatening situations were no longer occurring on a regular basis. It should have taken its place as an equal alongside the other faculties but the taste of power and control, and fear of the consequences should it do so, has made it reluctant to let go.

One clear way of identifying the workings of the monkey mind is to note the number of negative observations and commands that come up in the mind in daily life. Some familiar examples may include: "I can't/won't do that," "I've had enough of this," "That wasn't very good/nice/enjoyable," "He/she/it is stupid/no good/bad," etc. It is an interesting exercise to start saying just "Yes!" to oneself, and repeating it over and over, whatever thought or experience is coming up. Do this for five or ten minutes, saying "Yes!" either internally or out loud and, very quickly, one's whole energy starts to change, and one can start to feel lighter and happier, just by this simple affirmation of life as opposed to the usual denial of life. (Of course, the monkey mind may quickly come in as soon as you start doing it and say "that's stupid," but that is only to be expected!) The process of denial, saying "No!" may be continuing at a subliminal level, but this can easily be countered by the dynamic quality of the positive "Yes!" being overlaid on top.

Of course, we are still able to have good positive experiences and generally make progress along our chosen path, despite the influence of the controlling, monkey mind. Our ability to enjoy, in freedom from self-criticism (or the expected criticism of others), is a measure of the extent to which the monkey mind does not control all aspects of life. In the normal, healthy person, this influence is tempered and balanced by the other faculties, in particular the emotions and feelings, along with the expressed capacity for love, will, hope, joy, etc. These qualities will always be trying to break out, just as the outside world is always trying to break in. It is only in cases of depression, mania, negativity, and general self-destruction (and no doubt we have all been subject to them, to some extent, at some time) that we see the monkey mind operating without any counterbalance from the other qualities. In such cases, its hold has become so strong, its enthronement so confirmed and unchallenged, that no other experience can find a way in.

To continue the analogy, monkeys are also very quick and efficient thieves. When you are next in a wildlife safari park with monkeys around, place a roll of film on a table next to you. Given half a chance, they will snatch it up into a tree to examine it more closely. Just as surreptitiously and unceremoniously, the monkey mind has robbed us of our rightful inheritance as full and fully conscious citizens of the Universe.

Let us imagine a perfect state before the action of the monkey mind asserted power to protect the life of the individual through the "flight-or-fight" response. In this Garden of Eden condition (the Radiant Kingdom before Brains and Watchout took over), the world is harmonious and balanced, the essential unity of life is perceived and there is no sense of separation between the "I" and what is physically outside of one's self. The key word is identification—there is the sense of intimate connection with all things. Pain, and the fear bound up with it, is absent. All this changes with the realization of differences, when Adam and Eve realize their nakedness and know themselves to be different and distinct from one another. This is the point where perception of the world splits into two: we have subject and object, the knower and the known. From here it is a short step into all the dualistic conceptions of the world with which we are familiar—beautiful and ugly, love and hate, war and peace. This is the moment when the intellectual mind stops being the dutiful and obedient servant, performing useful functions such as selecting which fruit is most ripe to eat today and, along with the monkey mind, assumes control of the kingdom.

Everything is now seen as different and separate from the self. The illusory shell of the personality, or ego, starts to be constructed, with walls and defences to enforce the distinction between self and not-self. "Yes" and "no" are themselves two points of the subject-object split where, in saying "yes" to itself (as it must to support its survival), the ego says "no" to everything else. This "no" is the ego's most powerful weapon against the outside world, against change, against new experience, against anything which will rock the status quo.

To help maintain this control, the monkey mind has no respect for any values which do not serve its own purpose. It is completely without morals and impervious to values such as truth or beauty for their own sake. In fact, morality is something carved out to fit its own agenda. What works to support the control of the monkey mind becomes what is morally correct. Every kind of deceit can be employed and any course of behavior can be justified. All the weapons of the intellectual side of the individual, such as logic and common sense, are subverted to its cause.

Simply stated, the monkey mind's aim in every situation is to reinforce the subject-object split. Depending on the individual's personal agenda, this may be, for example, reflected in an underlying belief system that one is better than anyone else (arrogance) or not as good as everyone else (inferiority). Both viewpoints deny the fundamental equality and unity of life. Seen as part of an original requirement to decide on fight or flight, such perceptions may have once been useful. Carried into everyday life, as a program which exerts its influence over all our behavior, they can have a damaging long-term effect unless tempered with information from other aspects of our being.

Another important method of control used by the monkey mind is to make us forget our thoughts almost as soon as we have had them. How difficult it is to remember the thought we had two thoughts ago, let alone three. Swami Vivekananda, who revived Hinduism in India at the beginning of the century, wrote that the state of meditation could be attained if a single thought could be held undeflected for 12 seconds.[1] Whether or not the time frame is accurate, it is clear that continuity of thought is the enemy of the monkey mind and it uses this leaping around from one thought to another as a smokescreen to prevent us from really experiencing or knowing ourselves.

One way it achieves this is through the breathing. Each in-breath is followed, after a pause, by its mirror opposite in every way—the out-breath. Thoughts are very closely linked to the motion of the breath. For example, when relaxed, and thoughts are less insistent, frequent and demanding, breathing is slower and deeper. At the other extreme, there is hyperventilation, which is associated with the onset of panic attacks. Thoughts and fears rush in on one another as a result of perceived danger, whether from real or imagined sources.

If we observe ourselves closely, we will generally find that, in the normal way, each thought lasts only as long as an in-breath or an out-breath. Because the two breaths are so utterly different from each other, opposite in fact, it is very difficult to carry a thought across the barrier of the pause

---

1. Swami Vivekananda, *Raja Yoga* publ. Advaita Ashrama

between them. Our normal attention span, or the time we can concentrate on any one thing, is therefore very short, only as long as the length of one breath. As we move from in-breath to out-breath, our mind naturally moves onto another thought. Only the quality of the first breath, its emotion, for example—whether happy or sad—may be carried on it. This will be reflected in the next breath so the trend of thinking at any one time can be continued. A worried thought carried on a short, shallow in-breath will be mirrored by an out-breath of the same quality, the difference being that it is likely to carry a different thought. The second thought will carry the same quality as the one preceding it, with the added influence of random association. If the first thought was a worry about whether the cat has been fed today, the second thought may be concern over whether there is enough food in the house for the family to last the week. The two thoughts are connected by the random association of food and have the general stamp of "worried feeling."

Fortunately, it is possible to affect the thinking process by working with the breath, just as thoughts affect the way we breathe. Simply being aware of the breathing as it happens, in and out, is enough for the process to start slowing down and levelling out. As the breathing becomes less dominant, becoming slower and less intrusive, it opens the space for more awareness to be present. This awareness can then be carried across the divide between two breaths and we have the beginnings of concentration or absorption. Meditation is the cultivation of this as a habit.

Tracing thoughts backwards is an instructive exercise which demonstrates the randomness of thought patterns. As an example: you see someone out of the window who looks vaguely like someone you know. Then you remember who it was the person resembles. This makes you think of a particular characteristic, such as a big nose, which the person had. Then you start thinking of ways you have read about of operating on noses to make them smaller. Then you remember reading about a film star who had such an operation and this gets you thinking about a movie of theirs, in which they were driving a very fancy car. This makes you think of your own car and the fact that it needs servicing, so you immediately phone the garage for an appointment. The monkey mind is always using trivial features in a situation to hook your attention. In this way, it deflects you from the possibility of experiencing the totality of yourself and the world around you. These trivial features, such as the big nose, are the only links between thoughts. It is because of their irrelevance that one is often unable to remember thoughts one has just had. The random links between them have been forgotten exactly because of their triviality.

The monkey mind's fear of life in all its aspects is the foundation of its lust for power and control. Layer upon layer of justification and deception is woven into the personality to prevent the individual from recognizing this primary characteristic. As the layers are peeled back through the process of meditation or any other method of personal development, each block to full development throws itself up and, unable to resist the wave of truth coming towards it, collapses to reveal the next level. At the end of the process, we see the monkey mind as it really is—cowering in a corner, as trembling and fearful as a whipped dog. This is as far as it can run, and it can hide no longer. It is William Blake's painting of Nebuchadnezzar, brought down from the arrogance of his kingship to living with the beasts in the field.

Face to face with this aspect of ourselves, we need to bring enormous compassion to the way we deal with the monkey mind. It has, in its own way, always had our best interests at heart. Unfortunately, it has had to operate out of a very narrow knowledge base, with a limited range of reactions or resources at its disposal. Nevertheless, it deserves our thanks for the care it has taken to preserve us, life and limb. Its "no" has probably saved us from any number of accidents and misfortunes, as well as preventing us from achieving and enjoying more. Compassion is now needed because we need to retain its services as an ally. If we make an enemy of it, or frighten it too much, there is bound to be a strong reaction which will have the effect of allowing it to reassert its control over the individual. We want a democratic handover of power, not a coup. The monkey mind needs to be gently informed of its place in the kingdom of the individual soul, and provided with a detailed job description which lets it know the range of services required from it and when it may assert its presence.

Our Western background leads us to think that results can always be obtained by force, and that the mind can be made to concentrate on the matter at hand by the use of will power alone. In meditation, however, the mind is becoming accustomed to a decrease in activity. Trying to force it to stay still by an effort of concentration is counter-productive and will build up pressure. We are then more likely to experience headache than deeper levels of Awareness. Instead, the monkey mind has to be charmed and soothed into a less excitable state. The first result, then, is more restfulness and from this develops a widening awareness.

Krishnamurti stated that he was able to go for a three-hour walk in the woods and not have a single thought in that time. No nagging thoughts of "It must be time to go back," "What shall I have for lunch?" "I wonder how old so-and-so is," "Will I get lost if I take this path?" and so on. None of those thoughts which serve to take us out of the moment and prevent us from experiencing and enjoying just what is going on right now in front of our faces. Was Krishnamurti kidding us? Or was it simply a question of the controlling, monkey mind knowing its place, knowing its contribution was not required in this context of a gentle walk in the woods and not being so fearful that it could not lie down and take a rest itself, safely assured that, if its presence were required, it would be alerted?

From comments such as this from Krishnamurti, another great misapprehension has come about regarding meditation. It occurs in many books on the subject which maintain that the aim of meditation is to make the mind a blank slate without anything going on at all, a situation which would have more in common with deep sleep than pure awareness. Perceptions and feelings, the full activity of the hsin or heart-mind, are of course still present. It is just that a different style of functioning takes place in meditation, where the chattering of the mind is absent, but the single eye of perception is awakened. ("If thine eye be single, thy whole body shall be full of light." —*Gospel According to St Matthew* Ch.6 v.22.)

It is important on this adventure of discovery to understand that the Field of Awareness is not a vacant, empty, or negative state. This error has also come about because of the common misunderstanding of what is meant by the Buddhist "Void" or condition of Emptiness. The Void refers not to existence, but to substance and applies equally to the material world as to the transcendent world. All things and events are referred to as essentially insubstantial, in that they have no permanence, being transitory and ever-changing. It is empty in the sense that nothing contained in it, or the everyday world, has any abiding reality or existence by comparison with it. All that does not change is the Void itself, the receptacle, so to speak, of everything created and uncreated. An alternative description of the Void is *Tathagatha*, which is translated as "suchness" because it defies any more limiting definition. It could hardly be experienced by a mind that was completely blank!

5. AIMS OF MEDITATIVE TECHNIQUES

HE MONKEY MIND, THEN, with its constant chattering, its fears, and prejudices, prevents us from perceiving and enjoying the full potential of ourselves and of life as a whole. It works in two clear directions: inwardly and outwardly. Information and impulses from the environment surrounding us are filtered through a process of judgement which, unless modified by other faculties and stronger drives, prevents the possibility of enjoyment, opportunity and creative change. Inwardly, the monkey mind sets its agenda by a ceaseless chattering which both defines and limits the individual personality.

It has been so successful as far as the inner, or soul, life is concerned that even the soul's existence, or the possibility of any kind of transcendent life, is denied by most people. This is to be expected when the energies we are dealing with in our "interior castles" are so much more subtle and do not have the physical substance of objects and events in the external world. Imagine our hsin, our heart-mind, and all the other perceptive faculties as a house with many rooms, upstairs and downstairs, all fulfilling different functions. Most of the rooms are quiet, with nothing going on, or else so cluttered and dirty they cannot be used. In the living room, however, there is a group of monkeys leaping around and making a lot of noise. In addition, the radio, TV, and hi-fi are all going full blast creating a cacophony. All doors to the outside world are bolted and, despite a cold silence from the unoccupied upper rooms, the monkeys are trying to give the impression that a great time is being had by all or, at least, that they know best and are controlling the situation as well as can be expected.

Now, there is a gentle knocking on the front door, rather like Holman Hunt's painting "The Light of the World." It is the arrival of the Queen on the borders of the Radiant Kingdom—the still voice of the soul, calling to be allowed in, with the promise of mystery, happiness, and fulfillment. Most people or, in this analogy, houses, will not hear anything. There is so much noise and chattering going on they are oblivious to the invitation. Others hear something faint, but the monkeys, who are in effect running the show, refuse to let any new impulse in because they know it is likely to threaten their control of the situation. A few will hear the knock and be interested in finding out more. First, in order to pinpoint the source of the knocking, things will have to quiet down inside the house considerably. The knock may not be coming from the most obvious place, say the front door. It may be that, during their period of control, the monkeys have even removed all the doors and windows and bricked up the spaces. The one who knocks, the first chink of light pressing to enter, may not be coming from the place the householder may think the most obvious.

Quietness and stillness are essential. As the volume of activity is reduced, the potential for being awake to what is going on internally, can increase. Awareness increases in proportion to the quieting down of the chattering monkeys within. This stillness is the aim of all spiritual practices, not only of disciplines which involve sitting quietly. Dance, singing, and chanting all have this interior stillness as their aim. The Dance of the Whirling Dervishes is a good example. They take literally the idea of motion around a still point in their turning and turning. The focus is on the center of gravity which is always still and unacting, while the dance goes on around it. The motion takes up the attention of other faculties, such as the intellect and the chattering monkeys, and keeps them occupied and entranced in the moving, which is what they like to do. The deeper perennial aspects of the individual can then come more to the surface.

The use of the voice, especially in rhythmic chanting or singing psalms and hymns, can have the same effect. First the active mind is caught up in the process of what is being done physically, namely the expression of sound. More important, however, is the effect the chanting has on the breath. Oxygen, which is taken into the body on the in-breath, is an extremely volatile substance, a great and active mover of energy. The more active the body, say in running or dancing, the higher the requirement for oxygen to sustain that activity. It is also the chemical which sustains the activity of the brain, emotions and all other "active" faculties. On this basis, one can say that oxygen helps to keep us from experiencing our spiritual nature. What is needed is something which lowers our consumption of oxygen. In chanting or singing, intake of oxygen is reduced considerably in relation to the amount of carbon dioxide (CO_2) being generated. The focus is on the out-breath, which carries carbon dioxide into the atmosphere. The carbon, taken from our bodies, is heavier and slower than the lively, volatile oxygen. As it increases, relative to the amount of oxygen, the system's general level of activity reduces. Attention can then expand to include awareness of deeper levels. If the chanting is having its proper effect, it can be the same as sitting to meditate.

The physical inactivity of sitting meditation naturally demands less oxygen. A high intake is not required to sustain this level of activity. Breathing can become so slow and light that it may often appear to stop completely. The relation between oxygen and carbon dioxide changes until there is hardly any discernible breathing in and correspondingly only a slight expulsion of carbon dioxide. There is a relative increase of CO_2 to oxygen in the blood, which helps the mind to stay settled and prevent it from leaping about in its normal way. Sometimes, the two processes are reduced to such a degree that they seem to become one. This is what is referred to in the Bhagavad Gita as: "Pouring the in-breath into the out-breath and out-breath into the in-breath" (Ch.5:27). Awareness is then free. It should be recognized, however, that this is not a technique in itself. It is one effect or result of the meditative practice.

Prayer, which contains the ordered repetition of words, and other religious rites such as receiving Holy Communion, are designed to let the mind go free and, by quieting its more active tendencies, allow the meditative experience in. In Communion, the particular postures of the body, bowing the head, kneeling and cupping hands, all work to loosen the control of the mind and allow other energies and a wider awareness in.

Once this gradual process starts to unfold, the real business of meditation can begin—breaking down the bricked-up windows, cleaning off the window panes, opening doors, and knocking down boundary walls which have been built so high that no light or outside influence could penetrate. The overgrowth of the Forests of Illusion, which have prevented Reality from getting through, will need to be cut back severely.

This analogy of the house continues to hold good for the next stage of the process. To the awakening consciousness, the new influences of light and inspiration appear to come from outside the building. The individual everyday consciousness has become very circumscribed, in a literal sense. Everyone draws a circle around the limits of their understanding and their world view contains only what the mad monkeys allow to remain. When the shutters are allowed to open once again, it is under the impulse of forces which appear from the center to be entering from outside. At a later stage of experience, these notions of what is inside and what is outside take on a different meaning and it becomes relevant to question whether or not they are interchangeable or whether there is such a thing as inside and outside. No wonder the monkey mind is freaked out at the prospect of what will happen if control is given up!

Continuing the analogy further, it is not the intention of the new forces coming in to knock the house down completely or to knock it down to build a modern bungalow. The basic structure and design are sound—they are, after all, what makes our individuality—but it is true there may well be a need for some radical rebuilding, redecorating and general clearing out. The tenants have not looked after the place as well as could have been hoped. Inevitably money (time and energy) will have to be spent on renovations and improvements, particularly as the King is returning to live there.

REDISCOVERING
The
KINGDOM

6. THE FIELD OF AWARENESS

Just as life needs, in addition to the conscious waking state, an unconscious sleeping state, so, for man's self-experience is needed, besides the sphere of his sense-perceptions, another sphere also—indeed a much larger one—of elements not perceptible to the senses but existing within the same field where sense-perceptions originate.[1]

THE MEANING OF THE Sanskrit word *bodhi*, as in Buddha or bodhisattva, is "the quality of being awake or aware." The Buddha, therefore, is "The Awakened One." Eyes open, mind alert, aware. But, we ask ourselves, aware of what? In our everyday subject/object perception of the world, we generally use the word "aware" only in the sense of being aware of something. It is difficult for us to comprehend the notion of awareness as an absolute, the possibility of being aware without necessarily being aware of something distinct from the person who is "doing" the "being aware." For this reason, we need meditative techniques. If the mind could slip unaided from everyday thinking to pure Awareness, there would be no need for techniques. It is, however, important to understand their place. Techniques and practices are vehicles for taking us to the goal of expanded Awareness, in the same way as a car takes us to our destination. Once we have arrived, it can be dispensed with.

1. Rudolf Steiner, *The Philosophy of Spiritual Activity*

The meditative process is a movement of increasing awareness. This increase will, of necessity, be from within the dualistic subject/object field, because that is where we, as meditators, are starting. The monkey mind begins to quiet down and the *hsin* starts to make its presence felt: we have the beginnings of Awareness itself. At first, this transition is still taking place within the dualistic field. The meditator is aware of him/herself as separate and different from the object of meditation. By stages, this dualism is replaced by a unity of Awareness. But, for this to happen, both subject (the meditator) and object (the technique being used) have to disappear or, more accurately, be transformed. These elements are absorbed by the Field of Awareness and, with them, the concept of subject and object itself.

A kind of hyperspace has opened up. When Awareness is completely clear, it would be found to include everything created and uncreated with no discernible point as its center. The sense of individuality of the meditator is expanded to encompass the whole and all events within the Field perceived as taking place within oneself. William Blake said: "If the doors of perception were cleansed, everything would appear to man as it really is—infinite." It must be appreciated, however, that this cleansing is a gradual process. Like the cleaning of windows and opening of doors of the house, in the earlier analogy, the ability to let in light and the ensuing clarity will only develop over time and with effort. The monkeys, in their mischief, may well continually interrupt progress by smudging up the windows. It will be reassuring to remember that, just as the sun has not disappeared when it is hidden behind clouds, the Field of Awareness and the reality it represents are not lost just because they cannot be perceived through murky windows.

Awareness arises in the space between subject and object. The first purpose of whatever meditative technique we are using is to attract or charm the mind so that it can relax and the attention can be sustained on the object of focus. An element of continuity of consciousness, keeping the mind centered on one thing only, needs to develop, even if it can only be held for a few seconds. This concentration cannot be attained by trying to force the mind to stay still. The mind is always looking for something to get involved or absorbed in. It will always wander off to something more entrancing or into its own spiral of thoughts. When there is nothing of sufficient charm to attract, the monkey mind leaps off in search, as often as not without any real idea of what it needs.

So, something must be set before the mind to delight it. Our allies in this effort are the sense faculties. The senses do not have the outside world as their only field of operation. They can be developed and cultivated to work internally as well, and with a much greater degree of satisfaction. But it is not enough just to visualize a lotus flower. For the attention to be absorbed, the lotus flower must also be enjoyed, and enjoyed by all the senses—sight, sound, smell, taste, and touch.

Essentially, the use of the senses internally is still only a stepping-stone. Just as one seeks to go beyond the attraction of the external senses as a starting point in meditation, so one needs to transcend the inner senses to experience the pure Field of Awareness. Nevertheless, on the way, each of the senses can be enjoyed in its purest and most perfect form, allowing for deeper and more fulfilling perceptions and a range of experience that is not possible when the senses are projected into the external world. As one metaphorically travels back along the senses to their source, as in searching out the origin of a source of light, one discovers an integrated sense which can be described as the organ of spiritual perception. One possible type of experience is that of the senses exchanging their functions, so that one could taste sights, see smells, touch sounds, etc. This integrated sense is awakened. Developing this sense opens the door to perceiving the Field of Awareness. This experience of the inner senses is most delightful, entrancing all the faculties to the extent that the monkey mind is denied the scope to carry out its usual operations of sabotage.

The process of interiorizing one's experience until it touches its source is a progressive series of steps in non-attachment. A misunderstanding of this idea of non-attachment has led to the insistence in many religious disciplines of relinquishing all material possessions so that the spiritual can be grasped. Followers are encouraged to give up their possessions (or donate them to the guru) as if that, by itself, could take them nearer to enlightenment. The facets of the material world, such as cars and houses, are no more than things. Having them or not having them does not change what they are, nor does what we think about them affect them. From the point of view of spiritual experience and development, what needs to change is the concepts we hold about them and the values we place on having or not having them. For the Buddhists, it is primarily our concepts about the world which are holding us back from Reality and, hence, their insistence on the emptiness of both concepts and world. It is these elements in our conceptual world that need to be relinquished rather than the objects themselves. If you feel that your possessions are holding you back on your path, be aware that it is your concepts about them that restrain you and not the things themselves.

This concept-forming tendency does not apply only to the objective world. It can equally apply to concepts we may hold about "things and events" in the spiritual domain itself. For example, angels may or may not exist "out there," but making concrete forms and notions about them may hinder us. Likewise, hanging onto a particular experience or idea, whether gained through meditation, reading or teaching, and holding rigidly and defiantly to it through everything, may well prove a hindrance to further progress.

Fortunately, the gentle experience of meditation can guide us through these rocky waters and obstructive mental patterns will fade away in their own time and of their own accord. The one caveat, though, is that we continue to maintain and apply Awareness to the experiences and ideas that we come up with. What we think and feel, and how we act, needs to be finely sifted to establish its truth and integrity. Beyond a certain stage in this process, one can no longer gain help from books or teachers. One's own experience is the path itself, and each of us makes their own way along it. We become our own teachers and advisers so we must make use of whatever faculties we can to explore the truth of the way we are taking. The most valuable ally here is our discrimination, the ability to hold up our own experiences, as well as any teachings we may come across, and assess their "verity" in light of the highest we know to be true.

The Queen enters the Kingdom

7. Practical Steps

O UR STARTING POINT IS THE everyday self, its attention held by all the distractions of the material world, all being continually interpreted and pigeonholed by the monkey mind. Mental and physical activity is high, even in relatively quiet moments. From here, we need to proceed by degrees to increasing quietness and stillness. The heart (as an aspect of *hsin*, the heart-mind), which is responsible for driving the emotions, needs to come to rest. We must first begin, however, at the "gross" (in the sense of the most material) and from there move to the "subtle." The most gross aspect is, of course, our physical body and this must be brought into a preparatory state of calmness. A simple regime of *hatha yoga* or Chinese stretching exercises (*Qi Gong* or *Tai Chi Chuan*) will have this initial, calming effect and increase the body's suppleness. As the body is stretched through this type of exercise, it also becomes a better conductor and container of the new energies that will start to move through it in the meditation process.

Posture

From this a suitable posture for meditation needs to be taken up. The ideal sitting position is, without doubt, the lotus *asana* adopted by yogis with the back erect and each foot placed on the opposite thigh (full lotus) or cross-legged with one foot lifted onto the opposite thigh (half lotus). For most of us in the West, this is difficult either to achieve or maintain, and it should in no way be forced. The worst thing would be to ruin one's knees by forcing oneself into position before one is ready. Whatever sitting position one adopts, it should be comfortable. The main elements of the lotus position should, however, be noted—the back is erect and self-supporting, the chin is slightly tucked in to extend the top of the spinal column, and the whole body is steady. As the meditation practice develops, and energy starts to circulate better throughout the body, an improved posture will naturally arise, so this detail does not need excessive attention. Lying down is not recommended as there is a strong tendency to become drowsy and fall asleep. *The final word on posture, however, is that any comfortable position is suitable.*

Breathing

The next stage is the breathing. Simply by becoming aware of the breath, it will tend to slow down and become more even. In a number of systems, for example in Zen meditation, attention to the breathing is the only technique offered and may often be enough. As the breathing becomes less dominant, slower and less intrusive, the space is opened for more awareness to be present. This awareness can then be carried across the divide between two breaths and we have the beginnings of concentration or absorption. Meditation is the cultivation of this as a habit.

The circulation of energy through the body can be further harmonized by the following *pranayama* technique: breathe in normally holding one nostril with the thumb and then, removing the thumb from the first nostril and holding the other nostril with the middle finger, breathe out normally. Breathe in again through the same nostril and then placing the thumb on that nostril, breathe out through the other. Continue in this way for three to five minutes and the body and breath will be well relaxed for the start of meditation.

An important point is that one should not consider these preliminary steps as preparation, but see them as practice itself, in the same way that sitting for meditation is practice. We are aiming for a stage where the states of consciousness achieved in meditation become increasingly present in the rest of our lives. As they are firmly aware in the Zen Buddhist culture, everything one does, from washing one's bowl to *zazen* (sitting meditation) itself, is practice and none of it is seen as "preparation for practice." Such an attitude will lead to improvements in both the experience of meditation itself as well as in all the other aspects of daily life.

Stages of meditation

The *Yoga Sutras of Patanjali*, an ancient Indian text, define three distinct phases of the meditation process (Ch.3 v.1-3). These have the effect of taking the mind itself through its more gross to more subtle states. The first stage is *dharana* which is the mind (*hsin*) holding its attention to an object, say a flower. The eyes are closed, the attention is turned inwards, and one invokes the perception of a flower. All the meditator is aware of is the flower, nothing else, not even him/herself. At first the attention will wander off and have to be brought back to this object of meditation.

After a while, as the mind becomes more relaxed, the image of the flower will start to persist and some space will be created to allow the sense of one's self (the subject) as well as the flower in the same perceptual field. This is the second stage, called *dhyana*, where subject and object are perceived together and, by extension, the third factor of the relationship between the two, or the flow of attention from the subject towards the object.

The third stage, called *samadhi*, is when the "relationship between" has enlarged to incorporate both subject and object, and become the Field of Awareness itself. Only the essence of the two original elements (subject and object) remains, and that too may soon disappear, leaving only a lively perceptual field of energy and intelligence. This is the true meditation.

In the first instance, it will not be possible to hold the *samadhi* experience for any length of time—perhaps only for a second, if one is lucky. In order to sustain such completeness, all that is incomplete in one's life must be transformed. All stresses, darkness, frustrations, lethargy, inertia, angers, passions, etc., which are not consistent with *samadhi*, must go. Of course, they will not all go at once, and the extent to which they are there will prevent one from sustaining this state. It is often maintained that all one's stresses and imperfections must be removed before one can hope to experience *samadhi*, but this is not the case. The energy of *samadhi* itself is the greatest and most effective transformer of one's being. Even a small candle shone into a dark room will start to lighten it, though it may be some time before the room is bright and clean with all the dirt and debris that has collected in the corners completely cleared out.

It has been estimated that 90 percent of our conscious sensory input is through the eyes. For this reason, it is best to start the practice of *dharana* with a visual object, to help the hsin become absorbed in its own nature. As said in the previous chapter, however, the use of vision is not by itself enough. Seeing something does not necessarily bring us close to it. In fact, if anything, it makes us even more aware of the distance in between. Being able to see a tree on the horizon does not, of itself, create a sense of intimacy. For this to happen, the other senses need to be employed. Of all the senses, the most effective is touch. In *kundalini yoga*, touch is linked with the heart, and it is from here that our visualization needs to proceed. Imagine a flower, with petals of pink and white, green sepals and orange stamens and carpels. Move from seeing it to sensing it with the sense of touch from the heart. The heart will start to be moved and enriched, the colors perceived will start to deepen, and the attention will be more fully absorbed. To help build up a picture of completeness, one can then introduce the inner senses of taste, smell, and hearing. By active use of the imagination, allow the perceptions of these senses to come to you, for example by making the ears open to the sounds that are there, rather than by generating a sound in your mind. Each sense activity will add to the others to sustain the picture. Concentration is achieved, almost without effort, and the attention is held because the experience is by itself very enjoyable.

Without losing this visualization, the meditator starts to become aware of him/herself having this experience at the same time as being fully entranced by it. This extension happens naturally, without effort and is the beginning of the second stage of meditation, *dhyana*. This is in an important sense only an intermediate stage, as Awareness itself becomes the dominant feature of the experience and the original object of meditation, the flower, recedes in importance. Only the space, or the field in which it took place as an event, remains.

From this point, the meditator is, so to speak, on their own. The main definable experience is of absorption and a sense of fullness, characterized in some visual metaphor of light and energy. It may be experienced in the form of any of the artistic delineations, from Tibetan Buddhist mandalas to the stained glass of Christian churches, that have come down from the various religious and mystical traditions. Or it may appear as quite something else.

Techniques which make use of only one of the senses may have benefits up to a point but are unlikely to help develop and stabilize Awareness. For example, there are techniques which employ a *mantra* (a harmonious sound or series of sounds) sounded internally within the mind. This method has the potential of taking one very deep very rapidly, and will produce health benefits, such as lowering blood pressure, which naturally result from deep relaxation. There are, however, two main drawbacks to practices which use only the internally sounded *mantra*: by cultivating only the capacity for inner hearing, perception through the other senses is not developed and one's interior world will remain dark and, secondly, with the focus only on the mantra, the capacity of Awareness is not consciously cultivated and it will not develop of its own accord. This said, such techniques can be very useful for those beginning on the path of meditation as it does create the habit of turning the attention inwards.

It is very important to develop the capacity to visualize colors, forms, and space in detail and in three-dimensional depth. This awakens the faculty of Imagination which is, in effect, the sensory vehicle of Awareness itself. Imagination brings light to the room in which other spiritual events can be perceived. Without it, as in a darkened room, the same spiritual events may be taking place but, since one is not aware of them, they cannot be consciously experienced and used as signposts to further development.

The techniques which can be used for this type of visualization can be divided into two groups, though they can be combined as the meditator wishes. This is, after all, one area of life where nobody can tell you that you are not doing something right and it should be done in such and such a way!! One's own inner light is the guide here and you can test out various options to find what works best for you.

IDEALIZATION OF FORM

The first type of visualization can be described as "idealization of form" and can be used for creating pictures and scenes of ideal landscapes which one can wander through, either at leisure or as part of a search toward an undefined goal or grail. Calm lakes, mountains, and forests are best and the imagination can make these scenes really vivid. Experience the freshness of the air, its temperature and how it feels against your skin. Employ all your senses and faculties to enjoy your creation and make it real. Once created (the *dharana* phase), the scene will start to take on a life of its own as you, the meditator, enter into the frame (*dhyana*). The appearance of gentle, supportive, and sympathetic "friends," of human, angelic, bird, or animal form, should not surprise. Whether one chooses to see them as real entities which have entered your meditation to help guide you, or as aspects of your unconscious in Jung's terms, treat them as positive, beneficent influences which can lead you to deeper states of experience and understanding.

In cultivating a scene which absorbs all our sensory apparatus and fills our interior mental world, we are helped across that transition from one breath to the next and one thought to the next. Even though thoughts may wander off at the start of a session, the strength of the picture being built up allows the continuum of awareness to develop and be maintained.

This type of visualization is ideal for a guided meditation where one person is leading a group into the meditation experience. It is best if the leader does not attempt to define too clearly what the group should be experiencing but allow room for each individual to cultivate their faculties of Awareness and Imagination and create their own world.

PERFECTION OF FORM

This type of practice is more difficult to begin with though the transition from *dhyana* to *samadhi* is perhaps easier. In its purest form, derived from *yantra yoga*, the visualization centers on geometric or other symmetric forms such as the triangle, point, circle, square, pentagram, Star of David, etc. These can be visualized either in simple form or gradually built up to be highly complex. In traditional *yantra*, these symbols are often enclosed within lotus flowers representing the different *chakras* or centers of energy in the human body (see next chapter). These forms are not being treated as static or only symbolic. As with all else in meditation, one is working with energies and *yantra* practice is no different. The triangle, circle, square, etc., are representations of the patterns and forms which universal energy takes in the creative process. The intelligent source of creation, within Mind, separates in symmetrical patterns as can be seen in the cell mitosis of living organisms or the structure of snowflakes. (In traditional *yantra*, these symbols are also used in conjunction with mantras which are chanted aloud.)

Whether the "perfection of form" meditation is practiced using a symbol or something living such as a flower, the same attention must be given to using the imagination, allied to the interior senses, to create a lively world of feeling and perception.

It is best to select a visual object that is symmetrical, since the perception of contained symmetry gives the mind a sense of order which is craves. This makes it easier for the mind to relax and become sensitive to inner impressions which will also carry that sense of symmetry and orderliness.

There is plenty to hold the interest in this form of contemplation, as even the simplest symmetrical object, such as the point or circle, contains at least three elements: the two halves that divide along the midline, and the object as whole. This is the basis of the Christian idea of the Trinity of Father, Son and Holy Ghost (Mother), three-in-one and one-in-three.

The focus of meditation can be allowed to build up gradually, starting, for example, with a dot, adding a circle, then a triangle, to build a composite picture.

At the start of meditation, these geometric forms are seen only in two dimensions. In the transition to *dhyana*, they must become three-dimensional to take into account the space created in the "relationship between." With time, this transition to a three-dimensional image will occur naturally, though the process can be helped if one is able to visualize easily in three dimensions. *Samadhi* could then be understood, metaphorically and literally, as the fourth dimension of space.

The transition to *samadhi* is made by giving up the form of the distinction between subject and object, with only their essence retained. For this reason, the transition to *samadhi* may be easier using this rather than the "idealization of form" method.

Just as we started the meditation practice by paying attention to the breath, so when all techniques have been transcended, only the breathing is left. Breath is, in effect, the ultimate technique. Although it is offered as the only technique, along with correct posture, by Zen Buddhists, it would be very difficult for us in the West, leading active lives in a secular culture, to achieve results simply using this method. To start from breath alone will not easily create the opening for deeper experience. For this reason, additional deepening techniques are necessary, with the proviso that they will all, eventually, be left behind. Once the meditator has "gone behind the veil," specific techniques are no longer required and the meditation is led by its own dynamic.

By this stage of experience, the breath is likely to have become so slow and soft as to have all but disappeared. A state of such relaxation and quietness has been created that hardly any breathing is needed to maintain this level of activity. In this way, awareness of breathing becomes Awareness (*samadhi*) itself.

There is no reason why different techniques should not be used even within the same session of meditation. After all, the techniques are for the benefit of the meditator and not the other way around. After a short period of practice, some idea will be gained of what the meditation experience is, the direction in which the process is leading: increased sense of relaxation, greater calm, feelings of happiness are among the general indicators. On any particular day, then, in any one session, it will be possible to recognize whether a technique is "working" or not. If not, there is no reason not to try something else, even chanting aloud, which may better "clear the space" for deeper experience.

"UNSATISFACTORY EXPERIENCES"

Any time that strong sensations, such as headaches or un-pleasant thoughts and feelings come up, it is best to leave off the particular technique being used and, for as long as they persist, just be aware of the breathing process and of any sensations or thoughts that come up, without trying to change or influence them. When they pass, return again to the mantra and/or visualization.

Unpleasant sensations may come up for two reasons: a little strain from trying too hard has given rise to some tension; or a deeper level, pre-existing knot of stress has been contacted in the meditation and is in the process of coming out. As it filters through to the surface of consciousness, it begins to be experienced. One only needs to stay with the experience because the work on it has already been done— the knot has been loosened and is simply moving to the surface and out of its own accord.

An important physiological process is involved here which has, unfortunately, been widely misunderstood, causing many people to give up the practice of meditation. A typical experience might be that a meditator has a very deep healing experience in meditation early on in his/her practice. In subsequent sessions, it seems to them that they cannot "relax," "go deep," or "repeat the experience." If this apparent inability to meditate goes on for a while, they become discouraged and stop. What has happened is that, like someone tiptoeing through a herd of sleeping elephants, the meditator has gone right to the center in the first experience but, on returning to ordinary consciousness, has woken up the elephants, which then proceed to trumpet and stampede. This is experienced, for as many sessions as it takes to clear them, as turbulent thoughts and feelings, or as unfocused mental activity, which prevents the meditator from settling down more deeply. In truth, rather than stopping meditation, we should be very grateful for these "unsatisfactory" experiences as they are clearing the way for new and better ones to come!

These experiences are all part of the great renewal that takes place through meditation. The stresses and strains that prevent us from experiencing pure Awareness as a facet and feature of our daily lives are gradually worn away. They are like clouds obscuring the sight of the sun. The more they are removed, the more the sun can shine through and fill us with its warmth and light.

WHEN TO MEDITATE

Within a few sessions, it will be realized that the experience is never the same twice, and "good" experiences cannot be repeated, any more than "not-so-good" ones. This should not be surprising when one considers that we are dealing here with a dynamic world of life and energy. This world of deeper meaning and experience is no more static than our everyday lives, but changes and grows along with everything else. The spontaneity of the process is, by definition, not something that can be held or grasped and fixed in place.

Other additional factors will affect the type of experience we have. What one has eaten or drunk in the previous 24 hours, whether one is rested or tired, the impact of a whole range of environmental and personal considerations, will all have their effect. In order to optimize the experience of meditation, though, one needs to establish which factors are conducive to more effective practice and which are not. (The same factors will also be those, and this is no coincidence, which contribute generally to health and well-being.)

A regular rhythm of practice will be helpful in doing this. As far as possible, then, it is advisable to meditate at the same time each day, in the same place, and for the same length of time (15-40 minutes). There are two main benefits from this:

(i) Body, heart and mind get used to the idea of "going within" at this time, which helps to facilitate the process, and

(ii) By fixing these practical elements as a constant, one can more easily recognize which of the variable elements of one's lifestyle, e.g., diet and sleep patterns, are contributing to or detracting from the process.

One can, of course, meditate at any time and in any place. Catching a few minutes here or there, on a train or waiting for a bus, is no bad thing, but maximum progress demands rhythm and regularity as well. The best time to meditate is in the early morning when mind and body are at their freshest, and as a preparation for the day's activities.

At the end of the period of meditation, take five to ten minutes to lie down and relax. The mind may then wander off into a semi-dream state, or you may even feel you are floating. You may nod off to sleep for a minute or two. This is the time when the physiological and psychological changes wrought through the deep state of meditation fully integrate themselves into mind and body.

It is even more helpful if, during this time, one can briefly recall the events, sensations and experiences of the meditation period. It is otherwise easy to forget them, just as one forgets most of the dreams one has in sleep immediately on waking up. By recalling the meditation events in this rest period, which is a time of transition between the deeper state of consciousness and the everyday self, the Field of Awareness is brought more fully into our daily lives.

8. MEDITATION TECHNIQUES

I N THE PREVIOUS CHAPTER, general indications have been given on how to meditate, with various options on techniques which can be practiced. Below are suggestions for three specific techniques which can be used singly or in sequence, and combined with the practices suggested above. It is up to each meditator to take responsibility for the way they will practice, without relying on the pronouncements of "gurus," and develop their own methods in the light of their own continuing experience.

These three techniques all involve the use of mantras or sounds to enhance concentration (absorption) and the depth of experience. Even when a mantra technique is suggested on its own, there will be greater benefits when it is used in conjunction with other types of visualization.

The number of mantras is almost unlimited, many of them recommended for specific effects based on their meaning and sound value. They can be repeated out loud or internally. The practice of sounding a mantra internally is to allow it to become fainter and fainter within the recesses of the mind, almost as an echo of itself. It is heard more than sounded. In this way, the syllables of the mantra itself will change, lengthening, shortening, deepening, disappearing, or even changing into another sound altogether. These changes are to be allowed and enjoyed, and indicate that the practice is going well. In the same way, the picture created by visualization, whether a symmetrical symbol, flower or a fully formed

Buddha will take on a dynamic life of its own, changing, deepening, adopting different colors and become more vivid by its own dynamic. This is an inevitable development, as the "picture" moves from being an initial two-dimensional object to a three-dimensional one, and finally to an event in the "four-dimensional" field of samadhi. These changes are to be allowed and enjoyed.

Chakra meditation

The Eastern system of subtle physiology includes an understanding of seven centers or vortices of energy along the spine, known as *chakras* (Sanskrit for wheel). These exist in subtle matter but are believed to have a direct correspondence to the endocrine or glandular system of Western physiology. The relative activity of these *chakras* indicates a person's physical, emotional, mental, and spiritual state of health. Just as we know how the mind can affect the functioning of the body, the practice of meditation on the *chakras* leads to an improvement in their functioning and consequent benefits to health. The *chakras* have traditionally been represented in art, as well as for visualization, in the form of flowers. These images of flowers are used first for their aesthetic appeal to the senses and, secondly, because the petals of a flower and its general shape closely mirror the actual energetic activity of the chakras themselves.

First, take up a comfortable, stable posture and practice the breathing technique outlined in the previous chapter. Once aware of the gentle rise and fall of the breath:

(i) *Root chakra.* Visualize your spinal column and at the bottom of the spine, the coccyx, see a red flower with 4 petals. Perceive the color, shape, and texture of the flower as intimately and deeply as you can. Breathe in and, on the out-breath, sound aloud the syllable **LAM** for as long as the breath lasts. Repeat this three times, holding all the time the image of the flower. Notice, with the sounding of the syllable, changes in the color of the flower (deepening), its vibration or movement, the opening up of space around the flower in the area of that chakra.

(ii) *Sacral chakra.* Maintaining awareness of the root chakra, move your attention up to the second chakra, situated below the navel. Repeat the process, this time with an orange flower with 6 petals, sounding the syllable **VAM**. Attempt to see each of the petals individually.

(iii) *Solar plexus chakra.* Maintaining awareness of the two lower chakras, move up to the solar plexus center, seeing a yellow flower with 10 petals and sound the syllable **RAM**.

(iv) *Heart chakra.* As before, moving up to the heart chakra which is level with the physical heart, but in the center of the body. See a 12-petalled white and pink flower with green sepals and sound the syllable **HUM** three times.

(v) *Throat chakra.* Move up to the next chakra at the base of the neck and see a 16-petalled blue flower sounding the syllable **AH**.

(vi) *Third eye chakra.* This is situated between the eyebrows in the front of the head. This is the synthetic center of the previous five. The flower has two petals, each containing 48 petals within them, representing the positive and negative (from an electrical point of view) aspects of the total of petals in the other chakras. Visualize the color violet and sound the syllable **OM**.

(vii) *Crown chakra.* This highest chakra, known as the thousand-petalled lotus, sits above the crown of the head and is the true spiritual center, which only comes into full activity when all the other chakras have become harmonized and perfected. Visualize white or gold and keep silence for the same length of time maintained for each of the other chakras.

Sounding these syllables (mantras) out loud makes for a very powerful clearing experience. The practice can also be done sounding the mantras internally for a more deeply penetrating experience.

Chanting meditation

Om (c)- Ai (e)- Ya (d)- Ah (a)

A (c)- Ah (a)- Ram (b)- Ah (c)

First, take up a comfortable, stable posture and practice the breathing technique outlined in the previous chapter.

Center your attention in the heart chakra and chant this mantra aloud (the letters in brackets denote the musical notes which can easily be picked out on a piano, if required). After a few minutes repetitively chanting, stop sounding it aloud and continue to hear it internally only. This inner mantra can then be combined with visualization on a flower of perfect form and color located within the heart center.

The chant has no specific meaning (except for the Om at the start which in Eastern tradition represents the original creative sound of the universe). As the chant moves up and down the musical register from C up to E and down to A, it harmonizes and strengthens all the chakras. From C (heart), the chant moves to E (head chakras), D (throat), A (base of spine), C (heart) again, A (base of spine) again, B (solar plexus) to C again (heart). The repeated "ah" sound has the effect of opening and cleansing the chakras.

Internal mantra

This last suggested technique is recommended for internal use because of the sound's inward-going tendency, and its effect of taking the meditator to greater stillness and silence. The mantra, Hree, is a *kundalini yoga* mantra for the heart chakra, with the effect of bringing the meditator into connection with the characteristics of this chakra as the center of love and compassion. To underline the universal application of this mantra, it is useful to note that it is also the first syllable of the traditional Christian prayer in Greek, as in "Christ' eleison" (Christ, have mercy). A more accurate idea of pronunciation is gained from looking at it in the original Greek as Χριστε where the letter Χ is an asperated sound as opposed to the hard "Ch" of the English. It should be pronounced as if it were "Hc" rather than "Ch," with the sound rubbing against the palate in the mouth. This mantra is very effective at bringing the attention to deeper levels and holding it there, and is recommended for combining with any heart chakra meditation.

As an example: visualize a pink or pure white flower upturned within the heart center, and hear the sound "hree" vibrating within the flower. Once the flower is established in your imagination, bring in the other senses and experience the flower through touch, smell, sound, and taste as well as maintaining the vision of it. Each of the senses has a relation to a particular chakra: smell relates to the root, taste to spleen, sight to solar plexus, touch to heart, sound to throat, with the Third Eye integrating them all. The use of each sense will bring that chakra into activity even though the focus remains in the heart.

Then add, in the center of the flower, a flame, like a candle flame but brighter and more energetic. Visualize this flame as the active power of love spreading through all parts of you.

The heart desires and needs, more than anything else, an object to love. So, if you wish, place seated within the flame an idealization of the highest perfection you can imagine in human or "divine" form. This could be Buddha, Christ, or a figure without name out of your own imagination, embodying a perfection of virtues. Enter into relationship with this being, allow love to flow to you as well as from you. Above all, enjoy the visualization, and by touching your own deepest feelings in this way, you will come out of the meditation more fulfilled and refreshed.

APPENDIX

A BRIEF HISTORY OF THE UNIVERSE

*The Tao begot one, one begot two,
two begot three, and three begot
the ten thousand things*[1]

THIS IS A STORY WHICH TAKES
us back before the beginning of time, before the birth of
galaxies, star systems, planets, and other forms we recognize as
making up that quality called Life. In that unmanifest condition, the Universe was perfect, complete, and full in every
detail, except one. It did not know who it was. As a uni-verse
(a one-turning), it had no mirror to reflect itself and nothing
different from it with which to compare itself.

As the Universe then was, in its completeness, it was in
truth neither one nor none, for both of these are comparative
terms. As the *Tao Te Ching* says, it was simply the Tao, the Way.
It could not be said to be one, for that already implies the
existence of two. Two immediately creates three, which is the
relation between the first two.

Out of this aloneness was born a desire. The Universe
desired to know itself, to know what and who it was. Being
at this stage neither physical nor non-physical, neither light
nor dark, it nevertheless knew that, in order to know itself, it
would have to create something which it was not. And in

1. Tr. Gia-fu Feng and Jane English *Tao Te Ching* 42.

doing so, it would have to forget what it was. If it did not forget its essential completeness, it could not split into two. This ignorance is important first as a way of creating an opposite to the Universe's natural state of awareness and, second, as the starting point for remembering.

There was then the leap into dualism. Two halves each ignorant of the other and both ignorant of their common origin. Let us call them Spirit and Matter. As multiplicity continued, much as amoebae divide and increase from single cells, Spirit and Matter split up into an increasing number of units. The units of Spirit were gifted with the capacity for self-awareness or consciousness, the units of Matter were not.

The units of spirit became the original ensouling lives of humans, angels, and other beings characterized by consciousness. They were, however, conscious only of their little selves. The forgetting which had begun when the Universe first expressed itself as dual was passed into all subsequent divisions. Able to experience nothing except their own micro-universes, they began the long, tortuous road of remembering. Even with their built-in homing devices, it was going to be eons of time. And, as each slice of Spirit and Matter ploughed its own furrow of evolution back to its source, their distinctiveness and individuality was accentuated. Life had begun and already the journey home was started. The goal would be reached when each slice remembered its original identity as part of the Great Whole, and know itself again for the first time. Then the Universe would again be perfect, as it originally was, but with the added ability of knowing itself, as opposed to its earlier "unaware" state.

The goal of meditation is essentially the same as the goal of life on earth, which is for all sentient beings to know their essential nature and recover their wholeness. Insight into the underlying unity of life is gained to the extent that one realizes one's own wholeness. The totality of one's self is the totality of the Universe.

We are looking to recover that Garden of Eden state before Adam took the first fatal bite of the apple of the tree of (apparent) knowledge. He became aware of the differences in things, but no longer able to recognize their underlying unity. His awareness of his nakedness was the first realization of being separate, individual, and different. The Garden no longer existed for him, all he could see were differences and his own inability as a single individual to cope with or master his environment. With the loss of the sense of unity, he also lost his intuitive knowledge of how everything fitted together to make a whole of which he was a part. Hence the beginnings of ignorance and fear.

We clearly do not want a simple return to the state prior to Adam's eating of the fruit, a parallel to the stage in *The Radiant Kingdom* before the king was dethroned. We do not want to be aware simply of the homogeneous whole without diversity in all its different aspects. Daily life would become extremely difficult. What we want is the best of both worlds—to see the unity underlying the diverse, changing world around us and, at the same time, to be able to appreciate the diversity which has sprung from this unity. Meditation is the key to this process of unravelling the daily care, and removing the basis of ignorance and fear which comes from being cut off from one's heritage.

-The end-